Lady One

Lady One

of love and other poems

Breyten Breytenbach

Harcourt, Inc.

NEW YORK   SAN DIEGO   LONDON

www.HarcourtBooks.com

"The withering of the state" and "awake. after weeks" were first published in the *Paris Review.* "Revelation," "crucifixion," "mountain prison," and "mene mene tekel" were first published in *Salmagundi.* "Visiting the forefather's grave at Bac Giang, 4 December 1995" and "old light" were first published in the *American Poetry Review.* "Reading Li Bai" and "une vie sans ailleurs" were first published in slightly different form, and translated from the Afrikaans by Rita Dove, in the *New York Review of Books* and the *New Yorker* respectively. "John's night" was first published in *DoubleTake* magazine.

Library of Congress Cataloging-in-Publication Data
Breytenbach, Breyten.
Lady one (of love, and other poems)/Breyten Breytenbach.
p.   cm.
ISBN 0-15-100762-4
I. Title
PR9369.3.B67   L3   2002
821'.914—dc21   2001004457

Text set in New Baskerville
Printed in the United States of America

K J I H G F E D C B A

for Yolande

Contents

Lady One

the opening poem
("in the beginning there is love")

to her with the tiny feet like tamed pigeons
to her whose warm breath will be strung from your
  mouth
like the bunting of a pleasure cruiser
to her with the mother-spot a morning star
burning next to the scar under the breast
to her for whom the crest is a barely discernible sigh
to her with the black buttocks but purple flames
in the small of the back
to her who is the consort of a king enjoying you from up
  high
to her who is fresh snow between the sheets
to her with the slanted eyes and the bashful nether
  mouth
to her who laughs at your puny haft
to her who spits at your face in a foreign tongue
to her with the long gray memory and the wrinkles
the dim eyes and the initiate's know-how
to her who chases you away like a dog
to her who gurgles when stiffening in a jerk
like a body hanged from the rope of pleasure and pain
to her who takes all the Holy Names in vain
to her with the frog between the legs
to her with the pudendum like a green guitar
swollen and smooth
never yet plucked by a singing finger
to her who thought you had wings
to her with the pitch dark mouth and the powdered tits
to her who takes you for a dead lover
to her with the erotic hands

to her who killed herself
to her who murdered you
to her whose belly is a banked fire
to her who quite still turns her head away
so that you might not taste the tears
to her with the dorsal vertebrae like a ladder of notes
praying through the fingers
to her who relishes humble pie
to her who whispers unbelievable unlawfulnesses
in your ear at first
only to spout a sudden inkwell
to her with the brown body like a master violin
to her who talks to darkness
to her who like a snake
will let all of you slither down a smooth throat
to her who has forgotten you
to her who has never heard of you
to her for whom you write dedications like nuptial
    dances

to her, for all of her
this poem

the song of the cockroach (1)

Lady, oh Lady One—do I have a choice
Now the wind of forgetting
Blows me away into oblivion?
Can I speak, can I sing a song of beauty
In this theater and hope to be heard?
The worm of decay crawls over the face
Which only yesterday was fresh in the light,
Smiling, letting go the traces of night—
And death shall have no dominion,
I shouted. But the hand digging for the word
Of creation found a wound of bloody entrails
And plucked darkness twisted into a turd
As big as the sky sparkling with maggots.
Please deliver me, Lady, of prattle and cant
As I bury one hundred years of war and want.
And wrapped in my red flag of glory and culture
I shall bend a knee to the one-eyed Vulture.

autumn evening

at half-seven, after office hours
I lead my wife home by the hand
all along the banks of the Seine
over petrified pale bridges with dark wind in our hair
our clothes, across the river and teeth-chattering trees

and heaven shrivels to a swollen violet flower
the houses, the shops become blue and above
this city is the early nip of sweet-death autumn
as the windows open yellow eye by eye:
how wonderfully tart is my loved one's hair in the dusk

we shall climb the fifty-five steps to our room
and look at one another by the light of the bulb
to nibble on our frugal supper: sad bread, rice,
the meat, the wine, and with night in the bulging
        curtains
peel her dress over her shoulders, slip next, then the
        knickers

(I'm hooked on my little woman)
I'll drink from her tongue, like fire salamanders
we'll clamber on the bed
from the windowsill to the first gleaming roof-ridge
                        and then the moon

dark blossom

night long we lie listening to the whispering rain
the night rubbing against the panes is a dark blossom
I have the aroma of your flowering breasts in my nose
close your eyes
the earth turns so slowly
may night leak forever at the shutters
our bed is warm like a hand
I am so hungry
I am so thirsty
I am so sleepy
I have the scent of your whispering breasts in my throat
your body budding between sheets is a dark blossom
I am so stiff
how empty my eyes
come back long nights awake listening to chafing rain
come back what blooms at the panes is a leaking breast
come back the aroma of your whispering hands in my
    nose
open my eyes
I am so hungry
I am so thirsty
I am so sleepy
the heart that swells night long between ribs is a dark
    blossom
for you
close your eyes
open your eyes
the earth falls so slowly

dreams are wounds as well

thus every dream writes its small secret letter
in the morning we seek the scabs of ink in the mirror
to fold them away in archives

but the wounds do not heal

the darkest blood keeps blooming
orchards of revolution on sheets of the bed
or the bubbling of love in gardens

of wounds that do not heal

even the deaf dream melodies
as the insane whisper epistles
and the blind may look at the wind

pain bruises all we have a more intimate hue
how green were the birds in the garden
of my youth, how ripe and painted the sun

and the snow does not heal

the world is an emperor rich with people
the people are kings rich with trees
of fear or of hate, or trees of yearning

that dreams cannot heal

for *here* is our only eternal paradise—
we are rich as the fisherman is rich
when he sorts and counts his last eggs

and returns the fish to the sea—
to be able to talk as gossiping eggs
to sing like waves have so long bled

the blood that never heals

the soldiers have eyes like peas
the farmers have hands of soil
and they dream messages and dreams

filled with flowers which cannot heal

even a yellow parrot comes into the poem
airing its grievances from stanza
to line with the lament in the tongue's black sails

so that his song does not heal

so my nights will never heal or clot
because *you* have come to let my last blood
would you then be only a scar upon me?

without blood we cannot bleed
and our dreams are night's blood
as blood we are and dreamt in blood

just so I remain a bed marshal
evacuating my armies at night—
I press all the ink from my heart

for you, dreamt, who do not heal

our bodies are then sheaths of flesh
that one day have to dry as well, be sticks
when we, dreamless at last, go to sleep

for only then will the water turn to vinegar
and silence span its rainbows
and there our dreams will meet

and may these letters never heal
no, the words will never congeal

sleep little beloved

sleep little beloved
sleep sweet sleep black
wet like sugar in coffee
be happy in your dreams
play on flutes
buy a big house
eat the oldest pears—
those that sweeten in grayness—
sleep sweeter than pears

away with threats
away bastard wind
balls of rain the plundering sun
away hunger and lawsuits
away empty pockets
away all cancer
and toothache or narcosis
and sightless dogs
away empire of idiots
all but you
        and if you so wish
please me too

I shall watch over your dreams
I nail the flies to the wall
I lie in wait for the sun
        and the wind
        and the rain
if you laugh I will laugh
and if you weep
little love
don't you cry

look I'm buying you a hat
and fresh bread so black
new eyes and a coach
like pears in boxes
and music for your ears
and your hours
and crutches for your complaints
          and should you wish
America and the moon
for you I cut loose
my beautiful country

but that's tomorrow, *mañana*
first you must sleep beloved
sleep quickly, sleep far
sleep deeper than nights
and higher, lighter, lovelier
freer, more eternal
and happier than a feather

crucifixion

the old bull in the corral
tries to thrust horns all gray with age
into the shivering bellies
of grassgreen horses

but the trees full of birds
of my disciplinary song
force him to his knees
and the soil begins to bloom

for you I had only a handkerchief
embroidered with a bloodred heart
and when the birds with their bonedry scissors
cut the wind from the branches tree by tree

you tore the heart from the cloth
you tore the heart from my heart
so that your shoes might shine in the sun

why are you so dark my beloved?
why are the eyes in your head so black?

it must be all those nights
of sleeping by the fireplace of your body
it must be the night of our love
burning me so

around your shoes smolders horsegreen soil
and the lilywhite singer is nailed to the cross

the butterfly and the snail

that together we could tread the venus mount
together pick of your forbidden fruit
till apples hung like stars in the sky
figs are sweet, but love was sweeter

now your face rests happy as a butterfly
the flesh on a plate
where the prettiest nose trembles
like the nipple on a breast

and the moles on your sun-baked body
are sparse stars
over a brown heaven

your eyes large as shells rich with light would travel
to the sun where it sails between planets
figs are sweet, but love, but love

then to follow that sun as it flies
above cactuses over dunes
the snail's spiral house on froth
figs are sweet, but love was sweeter

your eyes look out of your head
like the cool deep windows
of a Moorish house on the day

because you
when you close your hands
the rosebud closes
and the butterfly tires

the snail in its shell is the nerve
in its tooth a life
below layers of fragile enamel
figs are sweet, but love was sweeter

we saw the summer islands so white in snow
and when we blew your foghorn
the sun was eclipsed by a snow of white wings
figs become sour, but love, but love was
sweeter than figs

—*Formentera*

the withering of the state

Many things will still change,
other flags fib and sing,
different ideologies may march—
geese look for water—
other people will straddle the globe,
perhaps the dogs will reign
and calculators make abortions an abomination

But we can whistle for it;
these cold fists squeezing
the juice from our heads
will also spurn deeper
(can the wind be stopped?):
the curs in their sputniks
will not prevent our discharge

I'll start wearing a hat
to keep in the dry goat,
you will ask for flatter shoes
for your waddling,
our eyes will shy away from light,
our nails and our skins grow slacker

Dear fellow mollusk, even a young wench
could not soothe the shivering
of King David's knees
(can the state eventually issue stoppers?):
where the mole campaigns
the most fanatic onion must mold

But one illusion will not wane:
even when we're hollowed
with all appendages, trimmings,
tools and props, our very lights crocked,
my toothless hand must continue
babbling in your deaf ear,
my senile tentacles
will want to delve on

So that at times,
as when we were young,
we may yet want to love again
with croaking throats

And perhaps then, as now, it will shrivel
to this old-fangled, let us say,
poem of state

rebel song

give me a pen
so I may sing
life is not in vain

give me a season
an autumn a spring
to see sky open eyes
when the peach tree vomits its white plenitude
a tyranny will be brought low

let the mothers weep
may breasts become dry
and bowels wither
when the scaffold at last is weaned

give me that love
which never rots between fingers
give me a love
as I want to give you one
my dove

grant me a heart
that will pulsate will beat
throb stronger than the white beating
heart of a frightened dove in the dark
knock louder than bitter bullets

give me a heart
small fountain of blood
to spout blossoms of joy
for blood is sweet
and beautiful
and never for naught

I want to die before I'm dead
when my blood is still fertile
and red
before I eat the black soil of doubt

give me two lips
and bright ink for tongue
to write the earth
one big letter
filled with the milk of mercy

sweeter day by day
spilling all bitterness
burning as summer
burns sweeter

then let it be summer
without blindfold or ravens
let the gallows give the peach tree
its red fruit of satisfaction

and give me a love song
of doves and atonement
that I may sing
my life was not in vain

for as I die
to wide eyes
under sky
so my red song will never lie
so my red song will never die

as of wings

Dearly beloved, I'm sending you a laughing dove
for no one will shoot a red message.
I throw my laughing dove high above
and I know all the hunters will think it's the sun.
Look, my dove rises and my dove goes down
and where it flies the oceans glitter
and trees become green
and it paints my tidings so red on your skin

For my love travels with you,
my love must stay an angel at your side,
like wings, white like the angel.
You must go on knowing my love
the way you have wings
with which you cannot fly

mountain prison

the mountain, so I imagine, fort where primeval shadows
can lie blackened from the light,
the mountain is full of herbs and old smells

nights when from the stronghold darkness comes,
the sweet breath of healing plants bruised
by an unsuspecting buck's hoof
or simply the unfolding of extinct flowers,
the temple-making, the hallowing wide

nights I have to think of you, exiled one,
that you cannot inhale this darkened joy,
can no longer be cured by deep sadness
and perhaps will have to choke on foreign soil

but then I think further: imagination
and memory shape one sweet mountain,
with clods in the mouth we are both
but gray recumbent possession

your tracks now cross over another beach
yet we each cherish the yearning for one
mountain-high fire
to purify obscurity and bring us to silence

mountain of alliance between you and me,
mountain of ecstasy,
mountain of appeasement,
bittersweet mount of irreality

—*Pollsmoor*

poem on toilet paper

nights everything is possible
this red labyrinth which I inhabit
    like a rat
its echoing passages and frown of steel barriers
  fade away
    only floodlights and solitary warders
ring the darkness in rising towers
  the jail becomes a monastery

from the bunk I take the pillow
and roll it tight
  this is my *zafu*
to the wall inside the sacred space
      I make *sampai*
deep in the ear coils the hollow pain
of the gonged wooden fish
and I cross my legs and my breathing
where I can see nothing
and nothing is seen
thus to turn back to reality

through walls the *mayas* break
spouting desires
      flames in the crotch
  burning images of the world
how deep will this land live on within me?
that the heart may never be blunted or blurred!
till the corpse is thrown on the town square
where curs flash their sweet fangs
and only turds paint the fields—
kill! kill that which has not lived!

21

it also pales
   the inner quad
becomes a haven for night birds
the moon has grown feathers
outside a tree stretches its roots
   to peer in
   and look upon darkness
where all is honed
   to a mountain of time endlessly unearthed

which recedes in time
   the wound closes up again
in this place I do *kin hin*
and listen to the breath which comes and goes
until it will stop coming
         to go

when light bleeds
I *gasho* to the wall
I sit in sun's snow
   and leave my chopped-off arm
     on the writing book:
       a flower to the silence

all around is jail
the way has no end
but what does it matter?

time

another hour another day and not one measure of time
can bring my heart to the bed where you lie
no half-end to living or the knife's slithering glide
through the fabric binding us
unwinding the rotting wind
neither darkness nor rage nor crazed knowledge
it is all a dream run dry

no war or peace or sky's shuddering fall will divide us
no night in cloak and hood and sheath of any kind
or city swollen up with knuckling stars
no power holds sway over our love

hold to your life, tiny butterfly
may my impotence cup you in all your flittering grace
beyond the traces of time's passing
contained like laughter in the sob
the white frame in dark sod
and wait, wait
if only for a while: another hour another day

like a baboon

Like a baboon I too grow gray toward eventime,
timid, filled with the fear of falling when earth
wanders from the sun and falls, continually falls
through endless trapdoors of flight: death
a flight-and-fall. How strange that senile and fertile
should mold so that death becomes a witlessness,
a hole for the windsock wanting to rhyme with life,
and that this which now has the green tongue of gall
in the mythical morning will whole the heel
and the eel, if words once more burn out in flight.

Leave the heart then to leak and the tongue to cyst—
I shall hide knee-deep in the poem,
because you know me, know that I am:
the midnight strangler, this fuckin' terrorist!

awake. after weeks

awake. after weeks of flashing heat
this morning when day broke
the heavens apart a wet bird
fluttered in to perch folded on the food shelf
in the kitchen. straight the lines
of silver water fall the walls stained rose
and greens burst in the inner courtyard
where stairs smell of horse.
light is the ocher color of earth
when the storm ends lovely.
lovely to lie abed hard
by the window fresh air Africa.
in Africa where blood blackens
and tiny desert creatures have to lick
the dew from their flanks to survive.
it must be like going to heaven
to jot down rain in Africa.

black memory

back from Africa
a clouded temple flower a dead bug
apricot-colored sand the grit of cowry shells
with the crushed susurration of groundswell
in your bag
and homelessness a slurry behind mooned
eyelids still dreaming to bag
gray monkey-bread trees as forests
of petrified fear

thus is raised writhed the tremor at the wrathful
thought of God:
dead boats washed up on the continent's white tongue
where people cowered with cross-beamed necks
to eye-write the man-eating
mirror of water

disconcerting thus
to cogitate a thing
and try to think a cure
for a suppurating love

mene mene tekel

some exiles
after a flamboyant trajectory of cocktails
die in the fetal crouch
with uncombed head in the oven
or fucked in a plastic placenta
and the posthumous note a white silence

sometimes I take to paper
as a blotted skin
smoothing mountains of deluded hope
to inner folds of words
at other moments it is one way
to cloak the pain
of angel footprints on the snowy slope

wallwriting
is always in a foreign tongue
in nowhere land

in nowhere land
I forfeited the pleasure of rhyme
and no longer trim the feeling to my hand
the moon's clockwork is a dead-eye watch

oh dark lady your body
a moving landscape of love as a lark
is no pleasantry
I do not court you for that final lay
your pardon is to stay the fear
which even the whitest blackout cannot cure
is there anywhere under the celestial sphere
a steadier cremation than soulfire?

take me now in my groom's garb of pulp
take the bumps and the breaks, the cape and the bull
as also this flourish of infinity as poem

revelation

The Ant took flight.
For a long time war was a rumor growling
beyond the desert's mysteries.
Further than skylines where the sun burns black
an army of youngsters vanished
to figure out a frontier.
But soon the garrison outposts were encircled one by
        one,
the capital's lifeline to the sea was cut
and black skeletons became specks before the eye
of the onlooker taking sight for too long.
When all about the night suddenly spat fiery tongues
and famished deserters in the outskirts
started trading boots and guns,
then the Ant, clad in his blue comrade's tunic,
fled southward.

We the people, relieved orphans, pushed from their
        pedestals
the prophets of a foreign all-knowing thought
and tore the idolatrous portraits from the walls,
giddy with freedom . . .
                        When all at once the barbarians
        were inside the gates—
bashful *Woyane* in sneakers and dirty coils of cloth
around the dreadlocks, or again
crowned with lions' crests of conquerers from the
        wilderness,
as of old high-stepping through history
to curdle the blood.

At the crossroads military vehicles
silenced by the manifold gray colors of sand
took up position, their heavy weapons
pointing to the four houses of breath.

First they took over the Mercato. The wireless
started prompting in an unfamiliar accent
deeper from the desert past.
Like birdsong. Our stray soldiers with the chopped-off
    feet
and all the twittering Secretaries from our Middle Empire
still fattened to a shine on hoarded food,
their suitcases stuffed with clean pajamas
and exculpatory secret files, were herded together
in fenced-in camps to be marked. A few comrade
    commanders
committed suicide. Harlots washed the scarlet
stigmata of bartered love from their faces.
And the city became a bloated bell tolling silences
with, behind walls, a muted stammering of speculation
hovering on the inaudible.

And at times the crack and deathshout of a former
    torture-artist
summarily dispatched in a dark alley.
Hard on daybreak beyond the bulwarks
the fireworks of yet another exploding ammunition
    dump would flower.
We asked ourselves whether this was the archangel of
    death
or perhaps the New Democracy. A revolutionary
    march-by of flames
chattered, hungry for news, through the roofs of shacks.
Under cover of a reddened dusk we heard hyenas cough.

In the morning we climbed up the black-scorched
        hilltops
with eucalyptus leaves in our nostrils
to confuse the giddy smell
of rotting corpses.
We stuffed veils in our mouths to suffocate the wailing.
For a long time we poked among spent mortar shells
and twisted metal, looking for a remembered identity.

"New Flower"—thus our city was called,
a labyrinth of whispers high above the sea's mirror.
But directives in the desert language
started staining our walls. In public squares
effigies of the new masters were hoisted to their feet
with the same omniscient eyes and flowing hair of old.
In courtyards of prayer places bearded bishops with
        miters
swung incense to yammer hymns about peace
and Solomon's seed coming to nest dove-like in Sheba's
        gorge.
Old men listened, leaning their chins on cleft sticks,
wrapped in shrouds. Flies, like ancient blood,
brought the movement of life to their lips. Young men
kissed the sanctified walls and doorposts, and the
        banners,
and later, with damp cheeks, also the conquerers' hands.

Survival is a rip-off of the past
and we can only think that which has existed forever.

On the palace gates the seals were broken.
The infinity of halls and corridors now repeated
the echo of beaten footsteps where dark murals
immortalize the Ant leading myriads of believers
against heathen and heretic and capitalist.
The heart-chamber of control had wall maps with flyshit
of multicolored thumbtacks spelling out a strategy
of resistance and final victory.
Here each general's chair had a red hammer and sickle
    on the back.
Pawtracks of the hyena.
On the floor there was a desert battlefield, an hourglass,
where miniature enemies were buried under historical
    determinism.
Just like imagination. Or memory.

And below iron doors, cloistered in the earth,
the emperors lay, each in his singular cradle,
clothed in the dusty sleep of ages,
their fingers burnt-out candles.

An innermost court: here the Empire's spindly talisman
languished behind bars . . .
                    Entoto, last of the royal lions,
named after the highest hill of our city,
smells powder and ashes
and meat gone blue, and in his eyes as yellow
as fires of glass
he captures one final glimpse
of that distant desert stillness.

the lament
(a ballad)

It's been so long since the red moon
Blew dust from the desert
As a veil to our faces
I remember the fold of your lips

Soldier, soldier, when will you return?

There are long months of mud
And days when the shivering air is white
Our seasons pass away
Sun scorches the harvest in the field
I have to find other pastures for the goat

Soldier, soldier, when will you return?

Earlier there were rumors of victory
In faraway provinces
But like the reports of defeat
They also blow away
Soldier . . .

Sometimes the bus brings
A stranger to town
With dead eyes
In his faded uniform

We are used to seeing
Stumps for arms and legs
Two hollows in the head
No one remembers the old war songs
The colors of the flag washed away in blood

Soldier, beloved, when will you return?

The child has grown tall
She has your eyes
Which see the wind
And when she cries
It is where I cannot hear
But she still gets happy
When somebody tells of a traveler
With neither name nor memory
Walking his footsteps at dusk through the lane
The hollow throb of long-lost boots

Soldier, soldier, when will you return?

I must sing in the bars
Though my voice is blue smoke
And at night at night
The groaning of my heart
Remembers a young body
So black and so hard
So beautiful so light
My face in the mirror is deaf

Soldier, soldier, when will you return?

Where is the letter with wings
Of my love
In your knapsack?
What is my intimate name?
In what foreign city do you wander
With hand held out
For the small change of forgetting?
I dream all the soft movements of your tongue

Soldier, soldier, will you ever return?

Or are there only rags
Of death over an abandoned field
The laughter of crows
The eternal smile turned to the sun
Your eyes your eyes
Which can see the wind?
Soldier, soldier . . .

Soldier, soldier . . .

island (1)

thus that island: hills shimmer where wind
wreathes blue tresses and shells the tongues
of olive trees planted a millennium ago
by Arabs, Carthaginians, Phoenicians,
seafarers and traders, invaders
from beyond a horizon

time and again the generations thrashed the trees
and pressed the oil
but it is long since profit was to be had
                              from the harvest
and moldy fruit litter the soil like gray wisdom teeth
—the figure of speech must grow its stone—
like phonemes run to seed or eyeballs
with all seeing extinct

wind constantly cultivates the land
oblivious to water and butterflies,
the mountains are dark glowing mirrors
ever and again reflecting invocations
                              of the silvery breath
and sand of ages skinned all the rocks
to penciled slate-slashes of repetition,
a rhythmical design of defective speech

depopulated, stark: here one sometimes sees
a black salamander sinister as a scarred left hand
signaling the sun, and where the skyline is a vision
a forgotten earthgod slithering through the breathing
      space
between naming and the memory of rot:
a blind Bacchus, a barren Pan, a blighted Gaia

bygone travelers already knew about decay
and clung to the sheath of life
or the mask of putrefaction:
a black knife was the insight with which the priest
could slit a long incision down the flank
to extract the cadaver's bowels
and fill the cavity with a learned concoction
of honey, beeswax, aromatic plants,
and the muttered prayer was a rhythmical speech
    impediment
to hush the shades

each coaxes his own landscape to growth
in interplay with the reasons of shadow and rest,
bed upon bed as stroked by the eye,
a vital vein through the priest's pulse
to mouth in the restless mumbling
                    of tides
and birdsong that never fades

and death then but an island
where it serves no purpose
to truss up the waters
and one surrenders to evisceration
as to a glooming of time

you! you! wherever you go you are my guide:
I see you sliding down the lip of luminous hills
and when light dies your hair turns dark

but more: abide me to follow you with the stirrings
of a heart searching for all the possible cadences
of our intercourse

for this is how a sun will be made
and liberated in the glimmer
how a shining hand may catch the black salamander

island (2)

"and nowhere innocence"
—M. Mooɪj

this island then, convulsions of sound
or dying stars, echo:
the *chaloupe* lowing from the fog
as night becomes light around a hollow throb
of deathshouts plaited into the stillness
of centuries when slaves were shipped from here,
and dazzling incandescence over the sea
smolders a darkness in memory,
and the throat a chaplet

the goats to be slaughtered
for the feast of *tabaski*
have tressed ribbons around their bleating necks
when children lead them to be cleansed in seawater
for the purification rites of animal transgression

the beasts to be quartered and hung
have ruminating eyes of reminiscence
like the imam with the blethering goatee rhythmically
lip-serviced by a cheeky choir of kids
in the Koranic school
behind leprous walls:
breathing is a string
of prayer beads flowingly numbered and strung
as the unnamable Names of One

braided as syllables of the unuttered Word,
winged on the wind, kites trill
a shrill design above court
and passage where beggars suddenly loom to hiss
and snap their empty fingers

then the incantation of drums tumble
down from the heights
where clouded survival artists live in lairs,
to impose a tone and woven pattern
upon the bay's slosh and kiss and silences

and nights when man and ewe slumber with staring eyes
rise again like a sigh from the haze
the hollow sough of tunnels sunk long ago
in the basalt to halter cellars of shame
to wharves of somber conveyance,
to keep the emptiness in abeyance

formerly time was forever,
now it is hollowed;
then thought and dream were seamless,
now they are ripped;
in those days there was history,
now only the suppurating cracks of consciousness
within the ocean's shimmering drowning

—*Gorée*

the request

When white metaphysicians stepped ashore on this
    continent
God still had a beard and a sex like lightning,
the earth was flat and time was for ever.
Now that flies as big as chickens are paraded
on leashes down the narrow alleys of our cities—
Is it right? Should it be permitted?
And the man (or was it a woman?) skinned, with face
rubbed away on the cement, nailed arse over heels
to the front door of the presidential residence—
Is it justified? Why don't you say anything?
And that baboon on the balcony having grinned a
    speech
who now wants to flap into the void—
Does it make sense? May it even happen?
And the nine-year-old orphans in the park
trying to unbutton the blouses of aged widows
asleep on the benches
to look for milk—
What do you make of it? Is it justified?
And all these swallows swooping, tearing the sky
like shivering steel arrowheads—
Answer me!

en état de mourir

to the colony to ignite a skyline
in search of selfhood
knowing that you will return home
with two hands of black fire.
the sentence slips into the paper
the way a snake slithers down its silence.
wind enchants the rooms.

perhaps we too are capable of dying.
perhaps this motherland will be sanded over
with white indifference.
history is heavy like the fingers on a hand.

to lie darkly whispering in the sea-eaten ear
of a ghostly past and a future cold sleep
and later turn the back of loneliness
upon one another
and regurgitate the silent name.

history is heavy like snakes writhing from sleeves.
wind enraptures the rooms.
natives are firebugs.

when you are old

when you are old and small and dressed in black
remember then again these dead moth words
against cold glass my love
even though you don't know the language:
I see you in the shadowy cowl
of the wall above the sea
looking upon the blue surge
till your eyes become water:
moths washed up on the beach
from a faraway locust-fed land
all night long stars throbbed
to the beat of guitars and singing
the thighs of another life
and the sun floats on bottomless waves
till your eyes become water:
the heart forever a refugee
a tower guard, drifter, hawker:
let your eyes go
and remember you too were once
a forgotten lover's
moth of landsickness
against the pane of a northern winter night

the poem of wisdom

listen, this is the sum of my life:
I traveled all the regions
where vitreous peaks are looking-glasses
for the absent face of God
and shadows were unknown there
except when whispering under the sods
and birds would plummet
to frozen sighs on the earth
and locusts loll singing
at the tables of kings
and through fallen cities where smudged flags
still fluttered for angels
to blow the soot from their noses
and in lands where hoarse democrats ruled
with iron fists
and distant districts where communists slurped soup
in the kitchens of masters
and everywhere everything rustled in the eyes
like maggots in the reading, listen

and flies all over,
and nowhere did I run
down a woman
with a horizontal pudent gap
or else her laugh would have gaped,
and death also

but to be underlined: flies and flies and flies . . .

John's night

journeyed through the sparkling day—
at first concrete city, then industrial dark suburbs,
    gradually
the countryside unwraps a newspaper of time and
    pollination—
green brushwood shadowed by white cattle—
what use is a landscape without shadowstains?—
windscreen splattered by dead insects like a page
of writing for the blind—in washrooms
of filling stations tattooed travelers soap their hands
and stare at themselves in the whore of the mirror—
to here in this town with its first roofs of baked clay tiles—
where men wear singlets—and it will get dark only
at midnight—in a tilted hotel room
looking upon a keep to the left and a garden enclosed
within stone walls—the hay has been baled, the fields are
    fair—
and sterner lines of hedges—each tree a whisperhouse—
somewhere far in the past fires flare—all about the scree
and peaks of quenched volcanoes banked blue against
    the sky—
fireflies burn softly—
quiet, quiet, quiet—
stay-over sleep with a rush of dreams—
tomorrow the morning cock, swooping swallows built
    their nests
under the eaves—breakfast of bread and butter and jam
and coffee—to drive on toward vineyards and olive
    groves—
cypresses are the torches of the dead, poplars bare-arsed
    light—
dream, death, keep moving my love—keep moving

bird farm

carried new mattresses to the upper floor,
dusted bedsteads, opened shutters
so that fragrant herbs may embalm the rooms,
looked out: I'm so proud of those hills
as if I'd drawn them myself

birds must be identified
and receive pet names, winds given direction,
trees need recognizable ills and boarders,
the hoopoe has a green bell in the throat

poured two fingers Bell's Old Scotch,
then locked the doors to keep all devils
out of bounds for the time being
and stoked the fire with chopped
half-dry tree trunks in the kitchen hearth
here we'll catch wind together,
grow old in another country

today I went down

today I went down on your body
while windows were thick white eyes
and hearkened the clogged cavities
in the small darkroom of your chest,
hedging an eternity over the aching voice
from your gorgeous throat,
agony and exaltation flow in one divide
if I may make so bold,
your thighs are a loveword your hair
night's glittering lining of secret disport:
I aimed for the innermost moon
and rent, moved by the syntax and the slow
of sadness and of joy, so
I love you, love you so

when the blinding comes,
the discomposure of silence,
it must be high up the hills
where hundreds of poor
stamp their feet in the dust, and drums
and woman voices like this ululating skyline
gag the final ecstasy

another country

seven o'clock and out in the field
with the farmer to bring water
behind the hill
the sun stains its burning to give cork oaks
an intimate darkness
and over the valley early fog lifts
to dew on the leaves and a clearer vision
north and south
every plant has its place
each hour its quarter in the day's workings
every word its own hollow
and love

northward to the border towering smoke
of brushfires bulge
crickets have nibbled some regions to the bone
and elsewhere it rained frogs
or an applause of butterflies
so that endless clapping darkened the hands
of people in rooms

nights the dreams are restlessly heavy with barbarians
in the south where flames leap higher by the day
of a summer which does not pass away
and love

seven-thirty the light lies silvery smooth
in the furrows dug by the farmer
to lead astray the drought
and bring succor to the runner beans,
the maize, tomatoes, melons, peppers,
onions, garlic, potatoes
and love

—*Can Ocells*

snow in a foreign night

a laughter of wild geese underlines predawn stillness:
it is going to be unholy
then as night's belly is slashed
a churning of white moths burns down more and more
to a skin of naked colorlessness
where direction and memory go lost

thus the book says:
the day man fashioned
from magic runes the first figures of writing
heaven and earth shivered
and gods and demons wept
for now the cunt of creation was bared

and three derived from two
show heaven and earth together
with the virtues of soil and sky
cupped by the two-legged one
who has a heart of emptiness:
the craving for birth written in white ink

white the letter I address to my heart
silent the syllables snow by the pane
neither death nor thought this day without you
shadowed by drapes the flight of wild geese
empty the stage of above and below
cold wings this last line of my dirge

—*Princeton*

after Celan

Carrying my share of snow
I crossed the border into darkness
and found people there. They all
called me "brother"

Once I overheard them sucking
                    burning tongues
to invaginate thoughts, about life
as our only shelter

And say: there is another world—
it is this

"Whorish othertime. And eternity
babelled around the edges, bloodblack"

then thaw

Then thaw:
squirrels scatter from the trees
to scrabble among moldy leaves
where snow's weak virginity
passes in dark water.
Footprints—yesterbirds frosted blue in death—
are wiped into patterns of absence
in the mind. Jackdaws yelp
in ever higher spirits from tip to ridge
and like scarecrows throw
all caution to the wind.

Too soon for spring:
subordinate clauses of soaked light
slick a ready tongue over the unexpectedly
blue bottomless sky.
The blackscratch shores of dank trunks
and khaki branches reach
for mirrorlife in the lake
clinging to its crust of ice
over dark water, clouded as old silver
or the aged smoke-prophecies of yesterday's dead
whorled in a swirl of cold settling.

When day flushes its pubic color
and the depth of distance is a closing shell
there still is the blurred background conversation
of sticks and stones:
then pale silence lipped over night's orifice.

the opening of the mouth ritual

then comes death:
you should be at hand
read out loud from the book
absent yourself murmuringly to make
believe true words will come
white in the mouth night
of the dier growing bigger
to retch outgasm
and then:

when breath shivers cold
when the rattle takes wing
you should lean forward with the finger
in a sacred gesture to insect
loose the tongue
a leap, curl, comma, sigh:

for then goes life
in voracious flight
from edge to hedge
to strip all the orchards
of memory
naked in song

visiting the forefather's grave
at Bac Giang, 4 December 1995

Wind from the North brings cold dust
to the city, the skies are gray—
today dragon-crested mountains will be invisible.
The route will take us to within a shout
of the Middle Kingdom
over bumpy roads along endless columns
of peasants with handkerchiefs masking nose and
       mouth.
Sampans are ticks sucked to Red River's broad flow.
Buffalo with the long gray shimmer of mud and ash
strain their furrowed pleats through wooden plows
       across mirrors
to turn over the sods
and stain red the water.

Everything must grow and live from the dying.
This is no-man's-land, always threatened by invaders.
Some houses are torched black,
and then there are soldiers with red stars on green
       cloth.
Flags slap the wind from tall bamboo poles.
A few natives know the odd expression or two
from beyond the border. Now and then
one sees an alien wordpicture stenciled
on a captured barbarian vehicle.

At the edge of the settlement
imagined by the ancestor and populated from his loins
lies the farm where his descendants still live.
Magic writesigns like the memory of moths against
    rafters.
A distant relative sucks black-faced on a hookah.
From the pigsty flies come swarming
and clouds close off the skyline.
The woman has black lacquered teeth,
the grandchildren are brimming with eyes.

In a nearby field his tomb is a threshing-floor
bordered by pawpaw trees, sugarcane,
sweet-potato runners. We arrange a bouquet of joss
    sticks
in a tin of rice, and the cold wind from the North
hustles the fragrant smokeshoots aslant
past the muttering of our remembrances
and our hands prayed palm to palm.

He lurks well here, first slip and seam
between stillness and the void. The arable plains
belong to the living, the dead
have taken to the hills.

On a knoll there's a pagoda blotted
behind a screen of bamboo and milkflowers.
The yellow walls are stamped black
by mushrooms of mold
and butterflies from a foreign tongue.
The gate is bolted and the graves weed-smothered.
We shout and hammer against the rotten wood of the
    door
but the deaf abbot with his gray unthoughts
squatting in the shrouded prayer hall
before the shining presence
of thousand-armed Kwanyin
will not hear our breaths behind the wind.

reading Li Bai

after the thick heat of day and the wet
heavy skies, after a day of sweat
so that we could taste the sweet salt
of each other, pearled in the groin,
after the bleat and blare of clogged streets
and gasoline stench and bright putrefied water
where the rower stood boated above his reflection

heaven trembled between the forked tongues of fire;
toilers trundled their burdens through the hours
or hawked baskets of fruit,
those fag-ended porters with charred footsoles
and a gnawing memory of food,
laying their numbed bodies down in darkened alleys
where rat and cockroach rummage in rubbish tips—
and they sing in their sleep, they sing their own dying,
for who will burn incense to their nameless faces
when they are dead?

the crown of the tallest banyan where the callbird keeps
    quiet
will shiver once in the breeze, the breeze will drop
    rustling
into the sighing branches of the guava, the red flame
    tree
and temple flower, sweet whiff of jasmine and
    honeysuckle
will seep into the courtyard, and later dark pearls raining
    down
to make of the street a mirror for the night

night is a mirror for an ancient letting go:
in a garden in this city you learned
how eternal the stirring of branches can be—
and always war slashing the skyline
and beggars without hands without legs
in their tattered green uniforms,
blood like old sweat stains the streets

when you song-sang your multiplication tables,
when each morning you inhaled the giddy afterthoughts
    of opium
in your father's empty study which all sleep long was filled
with the murmuring voices of yes and of no,
when your horse was a single stalk of bamboo
and you were so shy you dared not laugh
but traced with a finger shadow cracks on the wall
leaving messages for an imaginary playmate—
could you have dreamed that one day
I would write this dark sliver of mirror for you?

and when you were fifteen and began to comb your hair
    back
and stopped frowning your eyebrows, when you noticed
how yellow blossoms sifted down, dusting the roofs
like dead butterflies or flaking perfume,
quickly to look the other way—
what are the fragrant names of those trees?—
when floodwaters belched over the dikes and the forests
were poisoned by pollution and the fermenting meat of
    war,
always war, when the coconut palms stood empty
and starvation invaded the land—
could you have known that I want to be with you
like dust and like ashes?

those years of thick heat and wet
before I could show myself to you
were simply a journey to set out on
carefully, lest I stumble
in the mountain passes: I was on my way to you
and the monkeys' screech was smoke keening to heaven;
before your liberated house, the foundations leveled by
     freedom,
the traces of childhood games burn green as yesterday's
     gate
grown over with moss, and yellow blossoms
flutter like butterflies glutted on wind

sweat has made a wet moon of your sleeping face—
why should you weep for an old-old departure?
before you awaken, write me a letter
and I will come to meet you, even if the path is dark
leading deep into the past, all the way to Great Wind's
blowing sands: look, here on this page
you still canter the track on your bamboo steed . . .

—*Sai Gon, December 18, 1995*

hand paper

late summer evening: the skies
an inflammation beyond the Eiffel Tower,
stars begin to grunt in space
like the eyes of aircraft,
and I with my old body on the balcony
of this ancient building,
in the streets all about the city's rattle,
through an open window the tinkling of a piano,
a silence will come, pigeons look for night
in blue treetops in the park

how many evenings in eternity?
the present is but a past rippling outward
and everything else is indigenous,
through how many darknesses have we traveled thus
until a silence came and pigeons looked for night
in blue treetops in the park?
I'll go to the table and the light,
find the nighting of my hand in black paper

you are my lost time, woman:
you are my sweetheart and I am so glad

snow in Paris

and from darkness
still after many seasons
snow once again over Paris
this morning sheeting light
under gray blankets

sky damped down
all colors wet
whetted by a foreign tongue's
noiseless recollections
of etched lines vanished in much paper

chimneys smoke
a bird traces handnotes
of flight in the silently white
fresh Oriental verse
and a sleeve wipes it clean

shall we kindle the fireplace?
dream with our eyes in the flames
the hollows and dents
of words long forgotten
sputtering letter by letter in the sparks?

and go up in vapor
to flutter away
over the smothered roofscape?
shall we remember dead houses
and yet breathe love once again?

first light

first light washes in
froth on a dark crest
the dream still dawdles
with slow wings
your figure next to me asleep

brightness is a burnished blinding
the child in me remembers forgetting
a known world
where birds fly in and out,
the old human in me resurrects
with warmth in the throat
the child as unfamiliar
memory territory

how soft your body in the morning:
all of you one winged eyelid

will you own me still?
you open the balcony door
for the blind angel to stumble out
and fade away behind our seeing

everything a mirror
everything a mirror
we must meet again

the bridegroom's riding song

when it is moussem again in Imilchil
and the Imazighen descend
   from the frowning fissures of the Atlas mountains
to barter sheep for seed and salt
I will load mats and guy ropes on my keen-witted donkey
twist paradise flights in the lengths of my turban
with the patch in the neck
to show you how keen
I am about love
and ride stride-legged stride-legged through the gorge

when it is moussem again in Imilchil
where many tents as big as gulls
crouch with wings spread wide
around the mausoleum of Sidi Mohamed el Merheni
and pant in the breeze from the mountain heights
I will look for you
among the weaving bee-bodies of market-goers

search out your black eyes your veiled voice the
   whispering
flow of your silhouette
I want to learn how to read
the lining and stitching of your palms
let me buy you your bridal gown

my mountain buck my desert fruit

when it is moussem again in Imilchil
I will know you by the kohl of your eyes
your crimson cheek
the cloak of color over your bride-white robe

and at your throat the outgrowths of luck and good
    fortune
in silver and amber and blood-in-glass
for you have taken hold of my liver

the marabout's honey is a scripture in dust
you will rub a handful on your white-seamed breast
to ward off winter's pale nights with summer
and the pollen of bees
for I'm going to pay the qadi my ransom
and free of state and tribe and past
let my dust lie intimately with yours

tonight we'll grill the mechouï over vine-shoot embers
and suck between teeth the fat ewe's eye
the juicy udder and the ram's mountain clams
tonight we dance hunchbacked to the flute's fluttering
around flames flickering closer and clearer than stars

come back with me to my eternal bed of snow
behind white ramparts high on day's roof
where the fig tree murmurs its verse in royal shade
patterns
and pomegranates live like golden cheek-mirrors on the
    slope
and the heart of the well seeps deep black water
so you can show me how seasons rock to and fro
and the blossoms bloom all year through

for you have taken possession of my liver

be the stay of my tent my mountain fruit my desert buck
let me peel the bridal dress from your tattooed sweetness
and ride straddle-legged stride-legged to heaven through
64   the gorge

old light

official residence in Strangeland
where compatriots have grown white
with ham-tongued mouths and flowering neckties
and the ache of another country in the feet

on the wall a painting:
landshape somewhere in the Eastern Cape
just beyond sundown, a golden flow
brushed in behind empty hills
shifting towards erasure, a horse-cart
of silent passengers with stiff upper bodies
hatted in heathen respect for the universe,
the switch in the teamster's hand
                    is a dark slash
                    quote of language longing and fear
       unquote,
under the hooves of raw horses dust dove-thrashes
like light which has grown too dull
and must fall,
to the left and to the right is infinity—

love oh my love how lonely our world!

death in the poem

among spring clouds dark bombers spin
a boundary fence of dead sounds. female spiders
weave the things of their lust and hunger
into patterns of peace. *progress.*
the room of words is a cist for dreams

you wing over this holy earth
of evenings and patchwork sorrow
where blast furnaces spit acid tongues
and a discourse of soot. *prosperity.*
the rotten smell of dreams comes from the words

and governors crouch over arse-mirrors to frown
hairy fleshricks around the crown of the anus.
all time stands stiff within the chilly
embrace of death totally dismantled
to the tabernacles of language

the spectacle of hollow people
howling a blind humanness. people with sticks
beat other people or choke them
or slit their throats or burn them as one
would set fire to a blur of blackguards

no inoculation will ever protect you
from the moaning bullet. you wander for hours
through a vision of flames. your eyes are coals
your feet flake to ash in the animal park
where lion and camel and chimpanzee are consumed

bloody and cold the humans lie
under the clods and the grammar.
a plexus of extreme dread threads
history. and stare at you
with the mirrors of their eyes. *justice.*

everywhere woods are laid out for birds.
aged war criminals walk their Alsatian
dogs through the gardens and click
their tongues at modern decadence. in a cool bush
a nightingale chirrs her hinter-idiom

liberté. egalité. fraternité.
you are about to write broken verses like a mirror
of dark flight sounds just beyond
the border. now look the other way: *you die.*
but what if death will neither say nor stay?

—*Berlin*

in many countries at early dusk

In many countries at early dusk it is still dark
with the scratched writing of big trees
against the vault. Above this green night
vistas and vales of light shudder.
In many countries all the dogs are white
and trained to stifle their lament with rigid jaws.
The world's tribes turn out in wing and cowl:
politicians, the poets, the angels, clowns,
the jobless, Africans . . . Then there's a tight-eyed
      shivering
on variations of death as on a dark violin.

The word is the fruit of struggle. Imaginators kneel
begging for the gift of silence before a tower
where no god lives anymore. At other times
there are masters of the fruit crisscrossing
the land to verify the weight and the girth
of every woman's slitfig and put the findings to bed
all numbered in a black notebook.
Their fists are purpled up to the reach.
Birds are knotted to trees
with transparent ribbons.

The humble of the Republic have as task
the cleaning out of used tombs
for new investors. They may trade
the handfuls of black butterflies for personal gain
or swop them for figs on market days. There is room
for endless undertaking and their hands are dark
as far as the wrists. Activists wearing yellow ties
and pebbled eyeglasses sit behind tables
in white-tiled cellars where the walls
must periodically be hosed down.

In many countries on other occasions
statues are made to lie down with their faces
turned to the walls of lobbies
and their spines will be marked with the blindness of
      seashells.
Doubters bury blankets in the cool folds
of hills and sometimes the pawpaw trees
are smudged with snow. The People
will be the Party's capital. It is customary
to sing the alphabet with closed mouths
during the act of love when bodies rub together.

We go walking, love, after the wind in the mountain
where chasms brimming with the sough
of lost voices and the floundering
of birds hanged from the branches
fall away at our feet.
Expect nothing from Heaven.
If you get satisfaction from the ink of days,
of what will you then continue to doubt?
For in many countries in early evening it is still dark
with the pulse-writing of big trees.

sorrow heart

when you return it is already spring
in the city of dead birds,
a merle chokes on the burbling
spelling out of the territory of ruttishness,
chestnut trees have leprous green tongues
and dead-fire candles,
in bright daylight the moon parries blue clouds
to parade the speech of a cold shine
over shifting heavenly killing fields—
the heart is a songhill paraphing death
with its commas of make-believe breath stops

here is the letter of Ilham Rais
who last saw her father eighteen years ago:
airman sentenced to a desert
of lifelong agony . . .
after the failed *coup de peuple* against Hassan
of Morocco, after the tribunal, at dawn
August seven seventy-three
flown together with the other condemned
from Kénitra to hell's antechamber Tazmamart
and buried there
under paragraphs of eternity . . .

each a pariah veiled in the palaestra
of his own coop, twilight,
with no news ever of the soft
slide and dawning of day into night,
a closet without water . . .

five liters daily, drink and flush,
coffee and hundred-fifty grams bread,
a cupped hand of green peas or dry beans
and a bowl of boiled vermicelli . . .

the weight loss of years, the body evacuating
immunity, long since senseless, until it lies
down on the cement floor to palaver
one last time with decomposition
in the mumbling playing out
of pairing's terrain . . .

let it take place in camera,
warders forbid contact, food and water
pushed over the threshold, the door
locked, days are candles of dead fire
and the prisoner chokes on his words
as on riddles of parallaxes and parallels . . .

wrapped in his own blanket of shit
to the courtyard, in a ditch
under two bags of unslaked lime
sprinkled with water covered by dirt

palingenesis, from transcience
to the city of dead birds:
what else is the metaphor
but a pronouncement of clotted image-stillnesses?

Zibal

"What's unpronounced tends to nonexistence"
—Czeslaw Milosz

Perhaps we will end up here then
never to hear the swishing tails
of death's silk vestment:
Zibal, settlement on the hill.
We will move into that palace
propped against the promontory. Actually
but the shell of a fortress built
by grim invaders of another time
with cloths covering their faces to the eyes.
A fountain dribbles in the inner court
and on either side of the nightgate
now stained by the flocked shadows of a wild fig
are two giant statues:
an angel of wood and a dove in stone.
Heaven and earth thus mourned together,
there can be no parting between here and back.

The building is an enclosure
for goats penned in the vaulted halls.
In our dreams we lie listening with deep ears
to the timeless bleating in the passages,
the rustling of mouths ruminating saliva.
Up as far as a goat on its hindlegs the tapestries
are nibbled bare—mythical histories,
the portrayals of sackings and sagas,
flames fallen from the sky
have been crottels since the days of long ago.
And the nights.
On the last floor
are the remnants of a library. All fire,
my love, has fled from these verses;
what burned strangely are
neat little piles of ash,
an anthology in the empty garden.

Cinders will blow over the landscape.
From here we have a view on spotted olive groves below
awash in a silvery neglect, and the darker eddies
of carob trees no longer harvested.
As far as the faint, spittly sea—
a mirror always presents past time.
Some mornings we'll read the flight of the crows:
commas without words, for the land is bare
and all sense erased or peeled back to faded
      reminiscences.
Lower down there must be rock pipits
and cockamanders and voles and beetles and ants.
We see wind's wimple hooding our eyes
like a murmur, and hear the absences,
the raw remembrance.

People here don't know about work
for they are travelers, they'll say,
and watch us with unflinching eyes,
even though they've been around since the beginning
with a vocabulary which to us will crackle
like the cawing of seamews.

Will it be our imagination—
the skeleton with smoldering wings,
the man tied by snake to a tree,
and higher up the big supine bird
impaled upon branches?

In the dark interior we'll shelter.
Signs bruised against the wall are tracks
of earlier flames.
In the middle of the floor is the heap
of white pebbles where the Devil—
they call him *Robber*—
and the Prophet—known as *Cripple*—
argued all season through
about the intention and the finality of embodiment.
One for you and one for me,
one for now and one to be
and one forever.

For ever one. Here, with time, our smiles
will curdle to sneers, goat-eyes, small white stones,
a breeze of disputes in the wild fig tree,
swishing silk garments in the corridor.
As we go on loving one another.

the telling

tell me your stories
before they fade as we do
and our eyes are marbled with daybreak
as from lips in a smile of dust
the breath blows away
like the black slithering of the snake

tell me of the first time
you drank udder-warmed milk
where old-mouthed peasants
spoke a tongue you could not follow
and you shared your bedding with fleas

tell me how your mother
sent you as child
to serve a crippled vulture
in a house with closed shutters
and all the furniture shrouded in sheets
as white as the empty faces
of predecessors in the gloom

tell me you fell in love
in the dust and the sun
with your first bullfight
carnation behind the ear
blinded by the cocked back
and the shimmering suit and strut
of the matador

fragments, fragments:
tell me about distant lands
tumbling nights
hamlets in the mountains
grandmother a stickery of bones
garbed in brocade
and her mouth a darkened thought
when the words are blown

tell me of your estranged father's
garden dog in the tropical city
where you as black-white butterfly
had to singsong the lessons
of an ancient language
while forest fireplumes were spouting
wonderful fountains of sparks
and flashes shivered the hill-humped skyline

tell me the muttering deathbed
of your mother in that hospital
stinking of discarded footfalls
before these rumors
are invisible for ever
like the words of a child

people reading in these lines
a little here and a little tomorrow
all have their own ruminations
as shiftings of the heart
long since gone astray—
they know what you say
has been forgotten

tell me your rememberings
before they are snarled in a drawing of words
such as these which I must snare
now in a going away land

for already my memory is getting still
as a wind dies down
and I start shooting the black marbles
in a game whose rules I don't know

Urda

in that universe there was a stellar system tucked away
in the furthermost corner
and within this dying family a fire-plumed sun
with a string of planets
kicking up dust
like a cluck-cluck hen with chickens

and about the middlemost chick was known as Earth
blue and silver tumbler in space
overgrown with continents and seas
singing their bloom and their foam

among others the dark pear mothernamed Africa
a vast thicket world of light and distant hazes
and mosquitoes moaning around the ears
so you know you are human with feet in the clay
and look-above high the moon a mysterious mouth's
white tongue to lick your nights and your dreams
shiny and round

and all the way south lay Fuckland
with mountains as coxcombs reddening the pate
and flowers and poverty and grace and crap
and people begging for a glimmer of mercy
in history's cold-cold eye

and hidden up disappearance's sleeve
was a white-churched shanty-brown town
with wind the summer's breath
and chickens scratching in backyards
like poets attentively on the lookout for words
to rhyme with sob in the throat
and shadows in the orchard

and at the corner of three streets was a house
advanced in years all decrepit from tears
sloped against morning and doglegged against night
so that soon you had to see it was turning
turning its turning with time and tide
to become hide-away memory

and in that house a room
with floor made of creaking footsteps
and sighs like cloths
wiping the many faces of death
so that she may smile
at the maggot-madness of wanting to exist

and in the gloom a wardrobe waited
bread does remember the rustling wheat
exactly thus the fitment was home to a king's
tumbled tower of old-old stories

and in the top drawer the garments of generations
the lying-still movements kept in camphor

it was all there:
chrisoms and crape
crumpled cooing of lips
raiments for yesterday's faithful betrothal
and tomorrow's infidelity

and concealed under creases
of chagrin
this folded foolscap

thus, look, *here*
when stars jingle like empty milkpails
and the wilted moths pale
you must unfold and read
it for you
it's for you

"I love thee my love
like a thief in the dark
who could never refuse
the desire to steal from time
these hidden moves
of the writing heart"

Ithaka

Right at the beginning
when we were still slim
with answers as white as teeth and supple eyes,
and you innocent,
and my desire a snake mousing for your wrinkled nut—
right then and there I wanted to write you a poem

At the time the days were unthinking
and nights long enough to dream.
Time was for ever.
I scrabbled a spray of broad outlines on an envelope,
as ever at the outset
the shadows of one hand's displacements

I wanted to mark you with crosses
the way one flips a coin in the air
to conjecture the future,
play your body like a fresh instrument
unfolding under my fingers
to shudderingly sing of discovery's joys.
Thus, more or less, were the trails of the verse

which I could not knot to stanzas of sound.
And we lived, we traveled,
we bottled the seasons, explored the slits:
I squandered the dark dimensions

My errings put to sea:
the envelope as unwritten letter
sailed from one land to the other
from hand to hand.
Sometimes with a sudden dove of thrashing
in the throat
I discovered it again in a box of old papers
in the dark wind-filled loft of an evacuated house
and I tried to remember

what it was I would have liked to write
right at the beginning
when we were still lithe
with white-toothed answers and a supple eye

But the handmap had become
the pale membrane of a testament
scribbled in blotting language,
indecipherable like the snakeskin
no longer able to unknot
the deployment and pleating of desire
or to invent the whole

Now when my end is rising over the horizon
with bleached sails—
a first and last island
where only the blind dog waits in faith

I fold this writing in two, woman,
and lay it, hidden in the envelope
of a lost beginning,
like an unavailable homecoming
at your door

une vie sans ailleurs

but why does the heart still move
and recollect its darkened wings?
whence this wind from a silent sky
soundlessly shaking and stooping trees?
and the smothered cry
of bird ribboning black from the reeds
and all those blind houses
where the dying smear breath
to blur on the panes?
to whom does the color of the nightkeeper's coat
    matter?
since when are feathers blowing in the court?
what is the will of owning muttered
transcriptions of dusk
in the woman's eye the break of day,
the woman in the sun from the burdened branch?
how many dead rest and rot openmouthed in the
    mountain?
is there anything more that needs to be known?

all blood will dry and the ash of fireplaces
forgotten in earth's cold—
from the crackling forest of ice-blue stars
wind unfolds its scorched wings:
and of what will the heart continue to sing?

the song of the cockroach (2)

I shall bend a knee to the one-eyed Vulture
And wrap myself in my red flag of gore and culture
When we bury one hundred years of war and want . . .
Please deliver me, Lady, from this prattle and cant
As huge as a sky shimmering with maggots,
And pluck for us darkness twisted into a turd
Of creation. Show me the wound of bloody entrails
That I too may shout the hand digging for the word
Of death has had no dominion!
Smiling I'll let go of the theater of night
Which, only yesterday, was fresh in the light.
What? The worm of decay crawled over my face
In this shadow play and now hopes to be heard?
Can I speak, may I yet sing a line of beauty
To blow us away to oblivion
Like the wind of forgetting?
Lady, oh Lady One—do we have a choice?